DELIVERANCE

from FEAR

and from SICKNESS

by

ORAL ROBERTS

ORAL ROBERTS • TULSA 1, OKLAHOMA

Contents

PART I

PART II

Part One

DELIVERANCE
from FEAR

CHAPTER I

How One Man's Practice of Fear Paid

Off with Calamity

FEAR IS THE FORERUNNER OF CALAMITY. IT IS the creator of bad things. It is an attitude that brings the human being into captivity, confusion, frustration, inner conflicts and tension.

Psychologists say man is not born with fear. The Bible says, "God hath not given us the spirit of fear" (2 Timothy 1:7).

If we are not born with fear and God did not give it to us, where does it come from? Jesus says, "As thou hast believed, so be it unto thee" (Matthew 8:13).

We human beings are influenced by our believing. We have faith when we believe right. We have fear when we believe wrong.

Take the story of Job. He said, "The thing

9

which I greatly feared is come upon me and that which I was afraid of is come unto me" (Job 3:25).

What he feared, Job said, happened to him. It did what he believed it would do. He could not escape the results of his own fear.

Active fear is created by active wrong believing.

How did Job believe wrong? What did he greatly fear?

He feared that the hedge of protection around him would be destroyed and his good estate taken from him. The good things which a good God had

10

blessed him with wouldn't last. Something would happen to mar his happiness.

That is what he feared. That is what he thought about and came to believe. He became negative in his thinking and believing and filled his mind with fear. He doubted God's goodness.

There is a strange belief among people today that when some terrible calamity overtakes them, God is back of it. If they get sick, it is the will of the Creator. If they get in need, they are supposed to suffer want. If they do not succeed, that is their lot in life.

This is a throwback to the garden of Eden where the devil filled man with doubt. Man's first sin is also his present sin; the sin of doubting the Word and goodness of God. This sin is being cultivated by man. It has become a part of his thinking. When something terrible happens to him he says, "Why did God let this happen to me? What did I do to deserve it?" His response to the wonderful blessings God bestows upon him is, "This won't last. It will be taken away from me."

In his calamity he blames God; in his blessings he fears God will take them away from him.

This is practicing negative thinking in the worst

form, and it is directly opposite to right believing and the proper understanding of God.

While I was growing up, I was confused because I believed these things about God. Even after I was converted, this kind of believing plagued me. But, thank God, the Word of God enlightened me and gave me a new understanding of God's love and goodness. Since then, my believing has been steering me in the right direction for God's blessings to continually be upon my life.

The greatest discovery I ever made was the discovery that God is good, totally good. I made this discovery while reading the Bible. I never shall forget when I first read 3 John 2, Luke 9:56, John 10:10 and other similar Scriptures. They changed my thinking and put me to believing right. Take 3 John 2: "Beloved, I wish above all things that thou mayest prosper and be in health, even as thy soul prospereth."

God wants to save us, heal us, prosper us, bless us. This is His nature, His desire, His practice, His will.

He says, "The son of man is not come to destroy men's lives but to save them" (Luke 9:56).

He tells us that the devil is back of the powers that rob us of life and destroy us. "The thief (the

12

devil) cometh not but for to steal and to kill and to destroy," he says, "but I am come that they might have life and that they might have it more abundantly" (John 10:10).

God doesn't want to take anything good away from us but to add further blessings to us. The parable of the talents (Matthew 25:14–30) teaches us this. If we use the talents or possessions right that God gives us, they will be increased to us. Not decreased, but increased!

Job could not escape the results of his fear. It happened to him like he feared it would.

"For fifteen years," a famous preacher said to me, "I feared that some day I would be flat on my back both physically and spiritually. And in fifteen years I was flat on my back, exactly as I feared I would be!"

Laugh if you wish, but it is a definite fact that what you actively fear will ultimately affect your life.

Job's fear drove him toward trouble, and the day came when he was in such trouble he cursed the day he was born and wished he was dead.

Fear is positive. It is just as positive as faith is positive. It is powerful. Just as powerful in its realm as faith is in its realm. It is a product of wrong believing just as faith is a product of right believing.

Wrong believing is a reversed form of right believing, which means fear is a reversed form of faith. It is our believing-power used in the wrong way.

In other words, there is a believing that is faith and a believing that is fear.

The human being was created a free moral agent, and because of that, he is a believing creature. Being a free moral agent, he has to be a believing creature. There is no free moral agency unless he can direct his believing.

This capacity and power to believe is under the control of each individual. He can believe the way he wants to. His believing takes one of two forms: right believing or wrong believing.

A man gets into his car. He places his hand on the gear shift and puts it into the gear he wants it. The car obeys that gear, whether it is forward or reverse. The driver chooses the way the car goes. He puts forth the same energy and effort in shifting the car into reverse as he does in shifting it into forward.

The same is true in our believing. We use the same energy or effort to believe wrong as we do to believe right. The only difference is the direction our believing takes. When we believe right, our faith puts us in the right direction for the blessings of God to come to us and remain with us. When we believe wrong, our fear puts us in the wrong direction, filling us with confusion and panic.

CHAPTER II

How Right Believing Takes Away Your Fear

MY WIFE AND I HAD JUST BOARDED A PLANE IN Mobile, Alabama, to go to Jacksonville, Florida. We were fastening our seat belts when suddenly a man reached over, grabbed my right hand and shook it. I looked up just in time to see him disappearing up the aisle toward the front.

"Who was that man, Oral?" Evelyn asked.

"I am sure I don't know," I replied.

When we landed, this man came over to me and said, "Mr. Roberts, I am the man who shook your hand on the plane back in Mobile. I guess you are wondering who I am."

When I nodded, he said, "You will never know what it meant to me for you to be on that plane."

"Why?"

"Because you helped me overcome my fear."

"What are you afraid of and what did I do to help you?"

"I have a fear of riding in planes," he said, "and was I relieved to see you get on board! When I saw you and Mrs. Roberts getting on the plane ahead of me, I said to myself, 'This is one time I won't be afraid the plane will fall.' I was so thrilled that all I could think of was to shake your hand and hurry on to my seat. I was perfectly relaxed. I knew that since a man of God was aboard, the plane wouldn't fall."

"What difference did my being on board make?"

17

"Well, when I saw you, I believed the plane would be safe."

After talking to him for several minutes, I found out that he had built a great business through faith and hard work. His business carried him all over the nation and he had to fly often. Although he had used his faith to build up a great business, he had not overcome the fear of riding in planes. The faith he had in God to help him build up his business he laid aside when he boarded a plane. The moment he entered a plane, he quit using his faith. He let his imagination run wild. Every time the plane hit an air current and began to bounce around, he believed the plane was falling. He was beside himself with panic.

Yet, on the ground he was perfectly relaxed and calm. In the air, he was possessed with fear.

When he saw a man who practices his faith get on the same plane he was riding, he said, "It took the fear right out of me. I didn't see any reason to be afraid. For the first time I enjoyed my plane trip."

The wrong use of his believing brought panic, confusion and fear to him. When he began using his faith, he relaxed and enjoyed his plane trip.

When my oldest daughter, Rebecca, was small

18

and we left her with a baby sitter, the lady said, "You better be good while your parents are gone or those old ghosts in the dark will get you." Rebecca never had been afraid to go into a dark room by herself before. After that she wouldn't go into a room by herself.

When Ronald David came along and got big enough to walk, Rebecca would make him go with her when she had to go into a dark room.

Rebecca believed what the sitter had told her and it made her afraid. Through this kind of believing, she created her fear of the dark.

When she grew older and realized there were

no ghosts, she changed her believing and was no longer afraid of the dark.

The right use of her believing destroyed her fear of the dark.

Actually, fear is the absence of faith.

Fear is the absence of faith just as darkness is the absence of light.

There is an old fable that once a group of people came to the sun and said, "Sun, there is a place of midnight darkness on the earth where it is dark 24 hours a day."

The sun said, "I will go search for it."

The sun searched and searched but could not find it.

There was no darkness where the sun was.

Turn on the light in a room and instantly the darkness is gone. Turn off the light and instantly the darkness returns.

Leave the light on all the time and there is no darkness.

Why is this? Because light is dominant over darkness. It is dominant as long as you keep it in control.

Faith or right believing is dominant over fear just as light is dominant over darkness.

You can be totally free of fear when you put

20

your faith in control of your life and start believing right and keep believing right. As long as you believe right fear cannot dominate your life.

Faith is dominant over fear because it puts you in direct contact with God who is omnipotent. He scooped out the bed for the ocean, flung the stars from his finger tips, hung the earth on nothing, numbered the hairs on your head, knows your name, and cares for you.

Your faith puts Him in control of your life. He says, "I give you power over all the power of the enemy and nothing shall by any means hurt you" (Luke 10.19).

It is possible to live without fear because it is possible to believe right at all times.

Right believing gives you confidence because you know you are on the right track. It gives you the consciousness that providence is working for you. It calms your spirit, relaxes your nerves, gives you driving power and fills you with enthusiasm. People who believe right have great energy. People watch you and soon believe in you. They want to be on your side because everybody wants to be on the winning side.

CHAPTER III

How Job Got the Control of His Believing and Was Delivered from Fear and Sickness

ACTIVE FEAR IS CREATED BY ACTIVE WRONG believing. Wrong believing is the absence of faith, just as darkness is the absence of light.

Scientists say that it is the earth's relation to the sun which gives it its light. If the sun became inactive there are only enough light properties stored up in the earth for 72 hours of light. After that, the earth would be plunged into total and permanent darkness.

If the earth, apart from the sun, has only 72 hours of light stored up within itself, how long can the human being live apart from God before fear takes complete control of his life?

22

What happens to the soil when it doesn't rain? It hardens. When there is a prolonged absence of rain, drouth sets in and the soil is blown away. Active drouth is stronger than the rain that doesn't come. We are learning to conquer drouth by providing rain through irrigation.

What happens to the individual who doesn't use his faith, who doesn't believe right, who allows his mind to drift, to cooperate with everything that is negative?

When you plant wheat, what do you get? You get wheat. When you plant weeds, what do you get? You get weeds. When you plant nothing, what do you get? You get weeds.

If you believe right, what happens to you? You get good things, for faith produces after its kind.

If you believe wrong, what happens to you? You get bad things, for fear produces after its kind.

If you believe "just any old way," what happens to you? You get bad things, also.

Swing your believing in the direction you want to go and it will take you there.

This is what Job did. His fear had had a terrible effect upon him. He blamed his fear for what happened to him. "The thing which I greatly feared is come upon me," he said, "and that which I was afraid of is come unto me" (Job 3:25). Sitting in poverty, sickness, bereavement and loneliness he made up his mind to conquer his practice of fear. The formula Job used over his fear is age-old but as up-to-date as tomorrow. For it is God's way.

Here is the formula Job used:

First, Job admitted his fears.

"The thing which I greatly feared is come upon me," he said.

He was not too big to confess his fears.

He was not too proud to say he had been believing wrong.

He was not too stubborn to change his believing and start over.

He was not too selfish to blame God or others.

He put the blame where it belonged; upon his practice of fear.

Second, he came to realize that his faith was being tried.

"When he hath tried me, I shall come forth as gold" (Job 23:10).

Many things come against us to test us, to show us the kind of stuff we are putting into our lives. A trial or test will challenge you. It will polish you and bring the best out of you or it will grind you to pieces.

"The trial of your faith," the Bible says, "is more precious than gold" (1 Peter 1:7).

There was gold in Job as there is in everyone. There is that "certain something" that God has put in all of us.

It dawned on Job that he was being subjected to a refining process such as gold is. This is when he began to believe and practice faith in God. He said, "I believe God will bring me forth like gold."

25

Third, he turned completely to God, believing that his Redeemer lived and would deliver him.

"I know that my redeemer liveth," he said (Job 19:25).

It took effort for Job to say this, also great personal courage. He refused to take his troubles lying down. He refused to give up.

Look at Job in his miseries. Everything is against him. He has no beautiful surroundings or peaceful settings. There is no sublime mountain height, no glorious sunrise, no sparkling rainbow, no beautiful landscape, no lifting horizon. He is sitting in poverty, affliction, bereavement and loneliness. Nobody holds his hand or strokes his forehead or whispers encouragement or prays for him.

Yet he looks up and cries, "I know my redeemer liveth." He knew that somewhere there is a God who cares, that above the strongest storm the smallest prayer is heard.

Fourth, he accepted the fact that God has all power. "I know that thou canst do everything," he said (Job 42:2).

This is a literal fact: God can do everything. Not just anything, but everything. What a thing to know.

26

Job sat there in his miseries nodding his head and saying, "I know.

"I know I shall come forth as gold.

"I know my redeemer liveth.

"I know that thou canst do everything."

He was assailed by many doubts. His friends turned against him. It appeared that even God stood against him. But he had made his decision to believe, and he stuck to it. Once he cried, "Though God slay me, yet will I trust him" (Job 13:15).

A man said to me, "Mr. Roberts, if you will pray for me and God will deliver me out of this trouble I'm in, I'll believe in Him."

I replied, "You say you'll believe in him if I pray for you and God delivers you. You will never get it that way. Your believing comes first."

There is no deliverance until first there is right believing.

This is what real faith is.

*   *   *

Now the scene changes for Job, and God takes over.

Job has admitted his fears.

In the crucible of suffering he has turned completely to God, gotten control of his believing and swung it in the right direction.

Deathless words have poured forth from his feverish lips.

He has shown that everybody has gold in him or that "certain something" which connects him with God and which, if he will cling to, he will find the way to God for deliverance.

Finally he has reached the climax of his believing with his faith knocking on the door of Heaven.

What did God do? What can he do?

He can deliver. "And the Lord turned the captivity of Job, when he prayed for his friends: also the Lord gave Job twice as much as he had before" (Job 42:10).

Everything was restored to Job—twice!

The full values of life were given to him in double abundance.

This is what his faith caused God to do for him.

His practice of his faith put him in direct contact with his Redeemer who changed things for him.

As he believed, so was it done unto him.

He believed for deliverance from fear and its captivity, and he got what he believed for. He got

28

it in the measure he believed for it. In double abundance.

The abundance of life is exactly what Jesus came into the world to give mankind. "I am come that they might have life, and that they might have it more abundantly" (John 10:10).

Once a woman was brought to me in a wheel chair. When I came near her, she reached out and took hold of my coat.

"Brother Roberts," she said, "Look at me."

"What's the matter?" I asked as I looked at her. Her hands were knotted, her limbs crippled, her eyes bloodshot, her face strained.

She said, "This is what my fears have done to me."

As I looked at her I thought of Job's statement. "The thing which I greatly feared is come upon me, and that which I was afraid of is come unto me."

If I live to be a thousand years old, I shall never forget the look of despair on her face.

I said, "You can change all this if you'll just believe." She had confidence in what I told her and a light came in her eyes.

She said, "Can God deliver me from my fear?"

I said, "He will deliver you from your fear just like he will deliver you from your sickness. All you need to do is believe right."

She said, "How do I believe right?"

I said, "Repeat this Scripture after me: Lord, I believe, help thou mine unbelief."

She said, "But I believe in God."

I said, "Faith is more than believing in God. You must believe that God not only exists but that he will and does deliver you now."

She said, "Do you honestly believe that if I believe, God will deliver me from fear and heal my body?"

I said, "I know he will."

30

She said, "Put your hand on me and pray for me."

I prayed a brief prayer. She began to tremble. She said, "I believe I can come out of this wheel chair."

While I watched her, she immediately began to work her hands and body, and suddenly they were free. She rose up from the wheel chair under her own power and stood before me perfectly whole.

I saw this woman a few months later in one of our campaigns. She was radiant and beaming. "I have never been afraid again," she said, "since that night you prayed for me in St. Petersburg."

I replied, "and since you started believing right."

SUMMED UP

1. Don't expect deliverance from your fear until you believe for it.

2. Admit the fears you have and bring them out into the open.

3. Turn completely to God and believe that he cares for you and can do everything you need done for deliverance.

4. Practice right believing. Remember, the earth has light only as it keeps in proper relation to the sun. Your constant freedom from fear depends upon your right relation with God and the daily practice of your faith in him.

"Now it came to pass on a certain day, that he went into a ship with his disciples: and he said unto them, Let us go over unto the other side of the lake. And they launched forth. But as they sailed he fell asleep: and there came down a storm of wind on the lake; and they were filled with water, and were in jeopardy. And they came to him, and awoke him, saying, Master, master, we perish. Then he arose, and rebuked the wind and the raging of the water: and they ceased, and there was a calm. And he said unto them, Where is your faith? And they being afraid wondered, saying one to another, What manner of man is this! for he commandeth even the winds and water, and they obey him" (Luke 8:22–25).

CHAPTER IV

The Question Jesus Asks You When You Are Afraid: "Where Is Your Faith?"

FEAR IS UNKNOWN IN HEAVEN BECAUSE GOD is there. He is on the earth, too, because he is omnipresent. Therefore, we can conquer fear.

God is not afraid, and those who believe in him should not be afraid. Whoever has God's spirit in him has the spiritual part of heaven in him. It is the spirit that controls all things, even fear.

Jesus is with those who use their faith today just as he was with people who believed 2,000 years ago. One of the greatest examples of this is when Jesus stilled the tempest on the Sea of Galilee. He commanded his 12 disciples to get into a boat with him and go to the other side. They sailed away. They were happy and relaxed. Suddenly, a storm came up and they were afraid.

As the storm increased, their fear increased. Soon they were seized with panic and filled with wild imagination. They forgot Jesus and imagined that no one cared whether they went over or went under.

Although they had every reason not to be afraid, they allowed themselves to develop fear. Why? First, they forgot that Jesus was with them and, second, they failed to use their faith. The believing they could have used that they could not go under for going over, they used to fill themselves with fear that they couldn't go over for going under.

36

Their cry of fear awakened Jesus, who was asleep in the back part of the boat. He arose and stilled the tempest. When they reached the other side, he asked them this one question, a question that comes ringing across the centuries, "Where is your faith?"

They did not answer Jesus. Instead they said one to another, "What manner of man is this! for he commandeth even the winds and water and they obey him."

Jesus was seeking to get these 12 men to recognize their responsibility to use their faith during life's emergencies. Had they used their faith, they would not have become afraid. The storm would not have scared them out of their wits or caused them to go to pieces or made them accuse Jesus of not caring whether they lived or died.

Jesus' only reproof was, "Where is your faith?"

When I was in Israel, I visited the Sea of Galilee and took a boat ride on its blue waters. A man who has been raised on the shores of this sea told me that it is one of the most treacherous in the world. Situated 700 feet below sea level and nestling at the lowest point between the hills of Galilee and mountains of Gilead, it is subject to quick and violent storms. This man told me that when the wind shifts to the southeast and comes roaring across the sea, it takes only five minutes for the storm to strike the water with full force. He said in five minutes the sea, which has been calm all day, is whipped into sudden fury and filled with danger and death, and unless the ships get off the water, they are dashed to pieces.

Jesus knew this, and so did his disciples. Jesus knew, also, that faith is stronger than any storm. This is why he called his disciples aboard and said, "Let us go over."

This meant they couldn't go under for going over. Finding a quiet place on the boat, he lay down on a pillow and went to sleep.

No one can relax or sleep when he is afraid. Jesus believed they couldn't go under for going over. God held the sea in his hands. Faith was at the controls. Jesus slept

When the storm struck, the disciples forgot the presence of Jesus, also his promise that they couldn't go under for going over.

They cried, "Master, master, carest thou not that we perish?" By their wild cry we know three things about them.

(1) They believed they were alone in the sea and nobody cared.

38

(2) They believed they couldn't go over for going under.

(3) They believed they had no power to escape the storm.

The storm and its awful force, not Jesus and his power, was uppermost in their minds. Their danger, not their safety, was what they were thinking about. Their aloneness in the boat, not Jesus' presence, was the thought they dwelt on.

Jesus was positive in his believing; they were negative in theirs.

Jesus lay down, wrapped himself in the broad arms of faith, and went to sleep. Let the storm roar —he can't go under for going over.

The disciples forgot about the presence of Jesus and his promise. They became negative in their thinking and were soon like frightened animals.

Jesus had his thoughts under control; the disciples did not. He believed God was with him; they believed they were alone in the sea. He believed he couldn't go under for going over; they believed they couldn't go over for going under. He believed the storm couldn't touch them; they believed they would perish. He believed that everything was under control, the ship would get

39

through the storm and they would arrive safely on the other side, they were filled with hysteria and wild imagination. He believed the great spirit of God was hovering over them, protecting, shielding, guiding; they believed that God didn't care whether they lived or died.

The difference in Jesus' attitude that let him relax and the disciples' attitude that filled them with fear was in their believing.

In their fear, the disciples became confused. Not knowing what was going to happen next filled them with panic. They imagined all kinds of things.

Everything produces after its kind. Their fear bred fear. Jesus' faith bred faith. The disciples got more afraid; Jesus grew more confident.

When they came to themselves and remembered that Jesus was on board with them, they ran to find him. He was sound asleep!

What a picture this is. Every muscle in his body was relaxed. He was having no bad dreams. The thunder could not awaken him. The lightning could not startle him. The tossing boat could not disturb him. He was sleeping the sleep of the man who practices his faith in God.

The disciples were in the same boat, in the same sea, on the same trip, facing the same storm, in the

40

same circumstances as Jesus was. He slept, they wailed. He relaxed, they tensed. He lay down, they walked the floor. He believed God, they forgot they had a Savior. He believed he was going over, they believed they were going under.

They asked him if he cared what happened to them; he asked them, "Where is your faith?" They accused him of forgetting them; he reproved them for failing to use their faith. They screamed out their terror to him; he spoke quietly to them of their lost faith.

They acted like they had never heard of God; he acted like he had God. They forgot all their

41

previous contact with him; he remembered his daily walk with him. They were men who let their fear blot God out of their thinking; he was a man who filled his thoughts with God.

"Master, master, carest thou not that we perish?" they cried as they shook him awake.

Jesus arose, listened a moment to the wind, waded through the water splashing into the boat and stood at the bow.

Look at Jesus. The wind is blowing his hair and garments. The spray is wetting his face. The lightning is playing tricks in the sky. The thunder is beating its drums. The sea is raging and pitching and sucking at the boat. The long fingers of the storm are closing in.

Jesus doesn't flinch. He is not afraid.

Slowly he raises his hand. A clap of thunder roars across the sky. The lightning plays on the scene. The disciples crowd up close around him.

He speaks, his voice calm and resonant, "Peace, be still!"

Suddenly, the sea is hushed to sleep, the lightning fades, the thunder ceases, the waves fall away, the water is satiny smooth, there is "a great calm" and there is the shore.

They made the boat fast and went ashore.

Jesus spoke only twice. To the storm he said, "Peace, be still." To the disciples he said, "Where is your faith?"

The disciples were astonished. "What manner of man is this!" they asked, "for he commandeth even the winds and water and they obey him."

They could have said, "What a powerful thing faith is, for it commandeth the winds and water and they obey it."

In the light of Jesus' question, "Where is your faith?" (with emphasis on *your* faith), he means to tell us that our faith is the power that commands, the power that the storm obeys.

43

Jesus acted and talked differently in the storm than the disciples did. Why? He believed God. He did not doubt. He knew he could depend on faith taking them over instead of under.

Why didn't the disciples have the same relaxation and confidence Jesus had? You say, the storm scared them.

The storm did not create their fear. Their wrong believing did that. Jesus didn't say to them, "The storm made you afraid." He did say, "Where is your faith?"

The absence of their faith left them defenseless against the storm. Their feeling of insecurity made them afraid.

Absence of faith produces insecurity. Insecurity produces fear. Fear produces panic. Panic produces wild imagination. Wild imagination produces neurosis. Neurosis is only one step from psychosis. Psychosis is insanity!

Active faith produces contact with God. Contact with God produces confidence. Confidence produces security. Security produces relaxation. Relaxation produces balance. Balance is sanity!

Only faith is dominant over fear. It releases your power to believe right. Your right believing connects you with God and brings his power against

44

the storm. "Peace, be still!" God says, and the storm is gone.

You cannot wish fear away.

You cannot beg it to go away.

You cannot imagine it to be gone.

But you can use your faith against it, and believe it away!

How can your faith believe it away?

First, by remembering God. The disciples finally remembered Jesus was on the boat with them. When they went to him, they found he was willing to help them.

Second, by not blaming the storm or God for your fear. Jesus said, "Where is your faith?" Their faith was not hurled against the storm and that was why they were afraid. Failure to believe God filled them with insecurity and their insecurity made them afraid.

Third, by putting your confidence in Jesus. "What manner of man is this!" they said, "for he commandeth even the winds and water and they obey him." Seeing Jesus had such great power, they developed a new respect for and faith in him.

SUMMED UP

They came to a realization that they were afraid because they had forgotten God and were not using their faith.

They went to Jesus and told him their trouble. He responded to them and stilled the tempest. When in the storm, turn your thoughts to God. Remember his great power can set you free. Go to him and tell him your need of his help. Believe that he will deliver you. It will work! For you!

Remember, if you are afraid, Jesus asks you this one question: Where is your faith?

Part Two

DELIVERANCE
from SICKNESS

"And when Jesus was entered into Capernaum, there came unto him a centurion, beseeching him, And saying, Lord, my servant lieth at home sick of the palsy, grievously tormented. And Jesus saith unto him, I will come and heal him. The centurion answered and said, Lord, I am not worthy that thou shouldest come under my roof: but speak the word only, and my servant shall be healed. For I am a man under authority, having soldiers under me: and I say to this man, Go, and he goeth; and to another, Come, and he cometh; and to my servant, Do this, and he doeth it. When Jesus heard it, he marveled, and said to them that followed, Verily I say unto you, I have not found so great faith, no, not in Israel. And I say unto you, That many shall come from the east and west, and shall sit down with Abraham, and Isaac, and Jacob, in the kingdom of heaven. But the children of the Kingdom shall be cast out into outer darkness: there shall be weeping and gnashing of teeth. And Jesus said unto the centurion, Go thy way; and as thou hast believed, so be it done unto thee. And his servant was healed in the selfsame hour" (Matthew 8:5–13).

CHAPTER V

Right Believing—The Master Key to Your Healing from Sickness

WHEN I WAS IN CAPERNAUM RECENTLY, I UN-
derstood why Jesus loved it. It is a beautiful spot
on the western edge of the Sea of Galilee. Although
in ruins today, it is still one of the most delightful
places on earth.

When I walked among its ruins and stood on
the floor of the ancient synagogue where Jesus
often preached, I had a wonderful feeling. I felt
that I would like to remain there the rest of my
life. But one thing was missing while I was there—
the physical presence of Jesus. But any moment I
expected him to walk out and touch me.

When the centurion lived there two thousand
years ago, Jesus was there. Jesus loved Capernaum.

He later made it his home and the headquarters of his ministry in Galilee. It is said he never slept a night in Jerusalem or spent a day in Tiberias but he loved Capernaum. There he performed many of his mightiest miracles of healing and preached many of his greatest sermons.

The centurion was a Roman army captain who was stationed in Capernaum when Jesus was there. I envy and admire the centurion. He saw Jesus. He heard him preach, saw him heal the sick and even talked with him. As I stood where they talked and where Jesus responded to his faith, I turned and said to my guide, "I would give anything in the world if I had had the centurion's privilege."

The centurion saw Jesus. He saw him not as we see him today, not as tradition describes him, not as books picture him, but as he is. He saw a miracle-worker, a healer, a preacher of deliverance.

He saw a man who is not against anybody. He wasn't against the Jews. He wasn't against the Greeks. He wasn't against the Romans. He wasn't against anybody. He was against only four things. He was against sin. He was against disease. He was against fear. He was against demons. That's all.

He was for the human being. He healed by his

50

touch or his word, in person or at a distance. He told the people if they would only believe he would make them whole.

The centurion was so impressed by Jesus that he risked court martial to bow at his feet. And I can tell you that I will never forget the feeling that came over me when I knelt out there in the street where the centurion knelt before Jesus in the long ago.

The captain had seen the touch of Jesus' hand heal the most hopeless cripple and a word from his lips restore life to the dying.

He had seen that Jesus is more than man. His power is above all power. His authority is above all authority.

When his own trusted servant fell deathly ill with palsy and was grievously tormented, and the Emperor's physician pronounced the disease as being incurable by medical power, the centurion made up his mind to take his case to Jesus.

When the captain decided to go to Jesus and ask him to heal his servant, he knew he was doing a dangerous thing. The Romans hated the Jews. The captain might lose his command and even his life. He certainly would face ridicule. Sometimes it is easier to face death than ridicule.

51

In the presence of Jesus, the centurion lost his fears and found a new master. His first word was, "Lord."

He had never called man "Lord" before in his life except Caesar. He had never bowed to any power except Rome's power. Now he bows at the feet of Jesus and calls him Lord. What a spectacle!

This is force bowing to meekness.

Armed might before the unarmed.

The uniform of war before the seamless robe.

The proud eagle of Rome biting the dust before the Lamb of God.

A proud, rude, rough man saying, "Lord."

52

The transferring of a man's allegiance from man to God.

There in the streets of Capernaum, the centurion told Jesus about his servant and said, "Speak the word only, and my servant shall be healed." He believed that if Jesus would only speak the word, his servant would be made whole. Jesus said, "As thou hast believed, so be it done unto thee." And his servant was healed in the selfsame hour.

The centurion believed.

He got what he believed for.

He got it in the measure that he believed for it.

He got healing for his servant and a new master for his own soul.

His believing astonished and thrilled Jesus. He said, "I have not found so great faith, no, not in Israel."

The centurion's kind of believing is what Jesus says is great faith.

What the centurion did in the long ago can be done today. It is being done in tens of thousands of cases and with the same miraculous results.

THE CENTURION'S BELIEVING

A lot of people believe that had they lived in Jesus' time, it would have been easy for them to be healed. You would have been healed only if you believed. That was the master-key to healing then, it is the master-key to healing today.

There is no substitute for one's own believing.

Take the believing of the centurion who was a Roman army captain.

First, he believed that Jesus is the Lord.

He was not ashamed of this belief. He knelt before Jesus in public, looked up into his face and said, "Lord."

Because of this believing, Jesus said to him concerning his servant, "I will come and heal him."

Jesus made no effort to go and heal the centurion's servant until the centurion made him his Lord.

This kind of believing is what started Jesus in the direction the centurion wanted him to go.

When the centurion said, "Lord," Jesus said, "I will come and heal." The captain's believing moved Jesus to immediate action toward the healing of his servant.

54

While he was on his way to Jesus, he realized he was a sinner. All his life, Caesar had been his lord and master. Now Caesar could do nothing for him. He needed a new Lord and Master. When he reached Jesus he transferred his allegiance from Caesar to Jesus of Nazareth and called him "Lord."

Healing for your body is more closely connected with your soul than you realize. Healing is more than physical, more than mental, it is spiritual. It involves an act of your soul.

You must put first things first. The saving of your soul is the greatest miracle in the world. You must believe that Jesus Christ of Nazareth is the Lord, and believe in him as your personal Savior.

Your believing in him as your Savior will give you a change of mind, a change of heart, a change of thinking, a change of believing and a change of living. It will give you a new set of values and a new way of life.

This is a marvelous combination. The man said, "Lord." Jesus said, "I will come and heal him."

This combination has worked for centuries and it is working today. God loves you. He is waiting for you to make up your mind to make Him your Savior. His healing power is available to you.

Second, the centurion believed that Jesus has

55

power and authority over sickness and disease.

When Jesus said, "I will come and heal him," the captain replied, "Lord, I am not worthy for you to enter under my roof. Speak the word only and my servant shall be healed; for I am a man under authority, having soldiers under me. I say to this man 'Go' and he goeth, and to another 'Come' and he cometh; and to my servant 'Do this' and he doeth it."

Jesus was amazed. For the first time, he finds a man who recognizes his authority and power over sickness. The Army Captain is saying, "Lord, you don't have to come to my house for my servant to be healed. Just speak the word only and he shall be healed."

Jesus turned to the crowd and said, "Verily I say unto you, I have not found so great faith, no, not in Israel."

THE CAPTAIN'S FAITH

Jesus declared that this kind of believing is great faith. It is the believing that recognizes the power and authority of Christ over sickness and disease.

Up to this time, Jesus had found among his own people a blind disregard for his power and authority. They said, "He heals by the power of Beelze-bub, the chief of devils."

They failed to recognize that the miracles of healing he wrought upon the sick and afflicted were of God or that he healed because he had power and authority of God to heal. They declared his power and authority came from the devil.

For that reason, Jesus said, "The children of the Kingdom shall be cast out into outer darkness. There shall be weeping and gnashing of teeth." Jesus meant that those, who deny his power and authority over sickness and disease, blind them-selves to what God can do for them. As a result, they are filled with inner conflicts, unresolved frustrations and lost hope. The reason they don't get healed is because of their wrong believing.

God heals in many ways. He heals through good doctors, through medicine, through nature and climate, through understanding and love. Medical science in cooperation with the laws of nature has virtually wiped out certain diseases and is making great headway with others. The more they learn about the laws of nature and about the things God has put on this earth for the healing of man's body, the more they will be able to exercise the authority God has given them.

But there is a power above all power and an authority above all authority. There is a healing power above the doctor's power, or nature or climate or any other form of healing. That healing power is by faith in God. "The prayer of faith shall save (heal) the sick" (James 5:15).

Third, the centurion made Jesus' spoken word his point of contact.

"Speak the word," he said, "and my servant shall be healed."

The captain was accustomed to a different kind of power than ordinary men have. Being a military man, he was accustomed to issuing a command or speaking the word. He would say to this servant, "Do this," and he would do it. His spoken word or command was backed up by the power of Caesar and of the Roman Empire. This was one reason why he was able to recognize the power and authority of Jesus. He believed that Jesus had the power of God and the authority of God and that all the power and authority of Heaven and earth were back of his spoken word. Therefore, he didn't require Jesus to come to his house in order to believe his servant would be healed. Instead, he said, "Speak the word only, and my servant shall be healed."

58

This is something he asked Jesus to do to help him release his faith. If Jesus would speak the word, he would make that his point of contact.

The point of contact is any point where your faith makes contact with God's power. Any point whether it is the spoken word, the hem of Jesus' garment, the laying on of hands, or anything else.

The point of contact is important because it sets the time and is the point of expectation for your healing.

A beautiful example of this is the woman in the Bible who had an issue of blood and who made Jesus' robe her point of contact. "If I may touch but his clothes," she said, "I shall be whole."

At the point where she touched his clothes, she established her point of contact.

However, the touching of Jesus' clothes did not heal her. The point of contact does not heal. Jesus made that clear when he said, "Who touched me?"

She had only touched his clothes. Yet he said, "Who touched *me*?"

This means that when she touched his *clothes* with her hand, she touched *him* with her faith.

How did Jesus know that he had been touched?

He said, "I perceive that virtue (power) is gone out of me."

59

He felt healing power go out of him. The Bible says, "She felt in her body that she was healed of that plague."

The point of contact is actually a double release and a double feeling. When the woman released her faith, Jesus released his power. Something went out of her and something went out of Jesus. The woman's faith went out of her, Jesus' power went out of him.

The woman touched his clothes with her hand, believed him with her faith and immediately felt healing in her body.

The moment the woman's hand touched his clothes, her faith in him was released. Her released faith made contact with the power resident in his being and immediately he felt it go out of him. When she told Jesus what she had done, he was delighted with her faith and said, "Go in peace, thy faith hath made thee whole."

He was very careful to point out that touching his clothes did not heal her body. Her faith was responsible for his healing power entering her and making her whole.

The point of contact set the time for her to believe and was the point of expectation for her faith to take hold of the Lord and cause him to heal her.

60

TWO GREAT MIRACLES

Gladys Hanson of San Francisco, California, was a hopeless cripple and had been bedridden for many months. Her heart had collapsed. Her spinal cord was blocked. She had lost her reflexes and her equilibrium. Her side was paralyzed. Her lips were pinched on one side so that she could not speak normally. She had no feeling in the side of her face, arm, side, leg and foot. Her left leg had shriveled to about half the size of the other limb. Nervous convulsions swept through her body time and time again. She later testified, "My bed was my prison and the shadow of death was upon me."

She became a hopeless invalid and was brought home from St. Mary's Hospital to die.

In the meantime we brought our tent to Oakland, California, for a campaign. Gladys Hanson heard of our meeting through a friend who called her and said, "Gladys, people are getting healed at the tent. Will you let me come and take you there and see what God will do for you?"

Gladys Hanson was so sick and full of despair that she had lost her faith and was afraid to come.

Her friend kept calling her day after day until finally Gladys Hanson said, "All right, I will try it."

They carried her to the tent and placed her in a chair behind the platform in the invalid room. That was the night I preached this sermon, *The Master-Key-to-Healing*.

At the close of the sermon, I went back behind the platform to pray for the invalids. I prayed for several people before reaching Gladys Hanson. When she saw me praying for others she made a decision. She had heard me preach that night on *The Master-Key-to-Healing* in which I emphasized the point of contact. I especially emphasized it in the way that God deals with me. Although that was her first night to be present, she instantly grasped the significance of using a point of contact. Out of her desperate need and her new found faith she breathed a silent prayer. "Oh, God," she prayed, "let it be that when your servant puts his hand on my head, his hand shall be as thy hand and I will be healed."

Isn't that beautiful? I didn't know she had prayed this prayer. I had no idea what was going on in her mind. But when I walked up to her and started to pray, I knew that she had faith. I prayed the same prayer for her that I prayed for others.

Some of them had been healed and some of them had not been healed. I placed my right hand upon her head and commanded the diseases to come out of her in the name of Jesus Christ of Nazareth.

While I was doing this, which took only about five seconds, Gladys Hanson was doing her part. She was whispering, "Let his hand be as thy hand and I will be healed."

As I prayed, I turned my faith loose. When she felt my right hand touch her forehead, that is when she turned her faith loose. There were two people, a crippled woman and a minister of the gospel, with their faith meeting and being turned loose at the same time. In the flash of a second the healing power of God swept through her body. Suddenly, her body began to tingle with life. The numbness and paralysis left her side. Her lips parted. Her legs received strength and she jumped up out of the chair and stood with her hands up-raised, praising and magnifying God and with words pouring from her lips.

Then she began to walk around the prayer room and from that she went outside and began to run around the big tent, which is a quarter of a mile. She was instantly and completely healed. That night when she got home she was so full of joy

63

she didn't want to go to bed; however, in an hour or two she began to undress. She sat down on the side of the bed to pull off her hose, and when she did she screamed at the top of her voice. The leg which had been shriveled and paralyzed was restored perfectly whole and was the exact size of her other leg!

Today Gladys Hanson is preaching the gospel of Jesus Christ and telling this story from coast to coast.

Your point of contact won't heal you, but it will help you turn your faith loose. Faith, your faith, will deliver you from the crown of your head to the soles of your feet. Your faith has complete mastery over every disease in your body.

I prayed for a young girl one night in Norfolk, Virginia. She was about eighteen and had been born totally blind. I have not been able to bring healing to as many blind people as I want to, but when my faith is right and their faith is right, God heals them. This young girl was brought by her mother into the prayer line. She turned to me and said, "Brother Roberts, put your hand upon my eyes and when you do, God will let me see."

I knew this girl meant it. I knew that she had that as her point of contact.

64

I sensed that we were on the verge of a great miracle. I turned to the huge audience and told them what the girl said and asked them to have compassion.

I asked the girl if she had ever seen anything. She said, "No, not even my mother's face." When she said that, it broke me to pieces. The audience and I cried like children. I have never seen an audience so moved as they were that night. It seemed that the whole crowd was one person. I prayed a short prayer, put my right hand upon her blind eyes, commanded the blindness to go in the name of Jesus Christ of Nazareth. When I did, the presence of God came into my hand and I jerked it back. At that split second she turned her faith loose. Suddenly, the power of God came upon her, she opened her eyes and screamed at the top of her voice, "I can see! I can see!"

Her mother grabbed her and stood looking at her. Then the girl saw her mother's face for the first time. Her hands darted out and she took her mother's face in her hands and looked into her eyes. She began to shout that she could see her mother's face. The crowd leaped up and stood magnifying and praising God.

THE MASTERY OF FAITH

Getting back to the centurion again, let's see what he has done so far. First, he made Jesus Christ his Lord. Second, he recognized the power and authority of Jesus over sickness and disease. Third, he made the spoken word of Jesus his point of contact.

I am pointing out these things to you because it is important to know how to be healed. A lot of people want to be healed. The reason they are not healed is because they do not understand how to believe right. Then there are some people who want God to heal them regardless of their own believing. To them, healing is some kind of magic. You will find the master key to your healing is your own believing.

After the centurion had made these three steps, Jesus turned directly to him and said, "As thou hast believed, so be it done unto thee." The Bible states, "and his servant was healed in the selfsame hour."

When the centurion believed, the healing of his servant began that "selfsame hour."

When he believed!

66

Not when he performed some ritual or ceremony.

Not when he went through some religious form.

Not when he recited some so-called magic formula.

Not just through his thinking.

But when he believed!

When, through his point of contact, he released his faith.

The centurion's believing was completely responsible for Christ's healing his servant. His believing was his thoughts brought to a climax.

Had he not believed, his servant would not have been healed.

He believed that Jesus was the Lord, he believed that Jesus had power and authority over the sickness and disease in his servant's body, he believed that if Jesus would only speak the word his servant would be healed.

His believing did what Jesus told him it would do and what he believed it would do.

The servant was healed in the selfsame hour.

Do not underestimate your faith.

Do not seek a substitute for it.

Do not shirk your privilege and responsibility of using it.

67

Use your believing in the right way and as you believe, it will be done unto you.

You don't have to wait until you finish reading this book in order to be healed. Believe right now and as you believe, God will, in the selfsame hour, heal and make you whole.

SUMMED UP

Remember these four things:

1. The centurion was instrumental in the healing of his servant because he used his believing in the right way. To him, Jesus said, "As thou hast believed so be it done unto thee."

When you believe in the same way the centurion believed, Jesus will say the same thing to you as he said to him.

2. Remember, the point of contact does not heal, it sets the time and point of expectation for your healing. It is your faith or believing that causes God to heal you.

3. Remember Gladys Hanson who said, "Let his hand be as thy hand and I will be healed." When she released her faith, she was healed.

4. Remember the blind girl who said, "Brother Roberts, put your hand upon my eyes and when

68

you do, God will let me see." She made that her point of contact and through it turned her faith loose and received her sight.

Say this to yourself: "The master key to my healing is my believing. My faith has complete mastery over all the diseases in my body. Not just part of them but all of them and as I believe, I will be healed. Lord, I believe."

CHAPTER VI

The Healing of Little Willie Phelps

HIS HIP BONE WAS FLAT.

One leg was two and one-half inches short.

For four years he walked on crutches—since the age of six.

For four years he used a built-up shoe.

He could not run and play like other children.

Many times his little playmates would take his crutches away from him and leave him standing at their mercy.

For four years during Willie's school life the only way the school children had ever seen him was on crutches and his built-up shoe.

Willie's parents heard about our meeting in the auditorium in Roanoke, Virginia.

They told Willie if he had faith when Brother Roberts prayed for him, God would completely heal him.

70

Willie believed it.

Before they came, he made his parents promise that if he was healed they would go down the next day and buy him a new pair of shoes.

When they arrived at the auditorium, the building was packed and jammed with thousands standing outside.

They could not get in.

Little Willie wouldn't give up.

He said to his parents, "But I have just got to get in. Jesus is going to heal me."

Almost by a miracle he finally got in the auditorium.

There was no place even for them to stand. They worked their way back to a little anteroom.

This is where I entered the picture.

I had finished preaching the sermon, made the altar call and had prayed for the sick. It was unusually hot in the building because of the extremely large crowd.

I was on my way out of the building, tired, exhausted and wanting to get to my room to get some rest.

As I was passing by the room where little Willie was standing on his crutches and built-up shoe, I looked in this room. Why? I don't know.

71

I saw little Willie looking so lost and helpless.

Something got hold of me and I stopped and entered the room.

I said, "Son, do you want to be healed?"

Little Willie said, "Yes sir!"

I was too tired to pray, so I just reached out with my forefinger and touched his forehead, prayed a brief prayer in the name of Jesus of Nazareth for God to heal little Willie's leg, and then went out of the building.

A year and a half passed.

We had returned to Roanoke with the big tent.

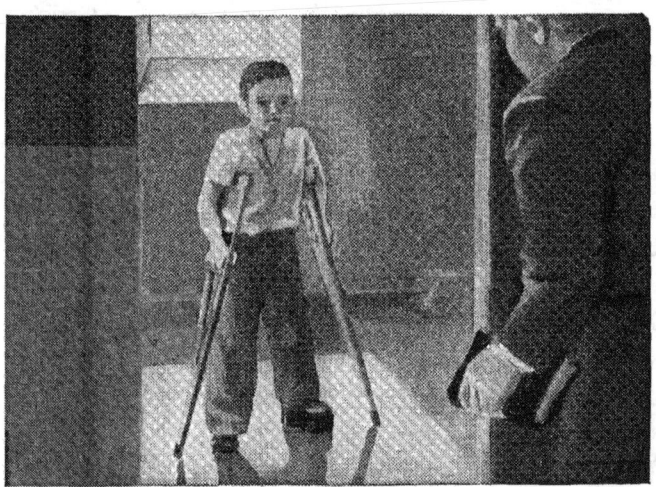

DELIVERANCE FROM SICKNESS

It was Sunday and ten thousand had packed the
tent cathedral with an overflow crowd standing
around the edge of the tent.

Brother DeWeese and Brother Braxton had little
Willie up on the platform before the people telling
his story over the microphone.

He was healed!

He had his crutches in one arm and his built-up
shoe in the other. His mother and father were
standing near.

The great crowd was thrilled as they heard his
testimony and saw him walk across the platform
carrying his crutches and built-up shoe.

Then Lee Braxton brought the parents and little
Willie to me and we talked while the photographer
took pictures.

This is what the parents and little Willie told
me:

The next day after Willie had been prayed for,
he couldn't go to school because he didn't have
any shoes that would fit him.

God had lengthened his leg the normal two and
one-half inches and the built-up shoe wouldn't fit
him. The mother took little Willie down to Lynch-
burg to buy some new shoes with normal thick-
ness so that he could go to school that afternoon.

73

He was late when he arrived at school, but when he walked in the classroom it almost broke up the school.

His schoolmates had never seen him except on crutches as he limped in day after day.

When he came up the aisle without his crutches, straight and normal like any other boy, the teacher said, "Willie, what's happened?"

He ran up the aisle to her desk and said, "Jesus healed me."

She said, "How?"

Little Willie said, "A preacher prayed for me and I was instantly healed."

The teacher said, "That must have cost a lot of money."

Little Willie said, "No, it didn't cost me a penny."

The teacher put her head down in her hands on her desk and cried like a baby.

This is what a point of contact will do.

My faith helped, but I am convinced it was little Willie Phelps' own faith that brought healing to his body.

I was extremely tired when I prayed for him. I merely touched him on the forehead with my forefinger and prayed a few seconds.

74

His parents had told him if Brother Roberts prayed for him and he believed, Jesus would heal him.

When I touched him and murmured my little prayer, this little boy believed.

Standing there on his crutches with tears streaming down his cheeks, he believed.

My prayer and touching him with my forefinger were his point of contact.

I sincerely believe that Willie's own faith caused God to perform the miracle of healing in his body.

In a glass enclosure in our office in Tulsa is Willie Phelps' built-up shoe and pair of crutches—a monument to the faith of a little boy.

CHAPTER VII

How to Get Your Healing When Others Are Not Interested in You

SHE HAD RHEUMATIC FEVER.

Her heart was badly affected.

She was in bed and could scarcely raise her arms.

Only twelve years old and she knew she wasn't getting well there in bed.

She knew Jesus could heal her. She had learned that through listening to our broadcast there in the Vancouver, B. C., area, where she lived.

She had faith, enthusiastic faith.

One day she heard on the broadcast that we were coming to Vancouver with the big tent. "You just wait until that big tent gets here," she said to her mother. "You can take me out there and Jesus will heal me."

Her mother had been listening to our program,

76

too, and believed God could heal, but she didn't quite share her daughter's enthusiasm. "But, honey," she said, "you know we can't let you get up out of bed."

"Mother, don't you want Jesus to heal me?"

"Yes, I do, but you are not supposed to move about. It will make your heart worse."

"Mother, you have got to promise to take me and I know Jesus won't let anything hurt me."

It took the little girl several days to get her mother willing to bring her to the meeting after we arrived. Finally, the mother and the girl got ready and the mother took the child and put her in the car and was fixing to leave.

Just at that moment a very close friend came up.

"Where are you going?" he asked.

"We are going to the Oral Roberts' campaign so he can pray for me and I can get healed," the girl said.

"You are what?"

"I am going to be healed."

The mother spoke, "What do you think about it?"

He said, "You can't be serious. Besides, you can't take that girl out there. She is likely to die on the way."

"But, Mother," the girl cried, "you promised me I could go and be prayed for."

"Well, I don't know what to do now," said the mother.

It seemed they would never get there that night. After this friend left they met other difficulties.

The little girl was determined, and they finally made it.

When the mother saw the huge crowd present, she was encouraged. She said, "If so many people believe God can heal, surely we are in the right place."

Still she had some misgivings.

The little girl was bubbling over with enthusiasm.

After finishing the message, I went back in the invalid room to pray for the emergency cases when I saw this child. They told me what was wrong with her.

"Put your hand on your heart, honey," I said.

I placed my hand over hers.

Her heart was pounding wildly.

Her body was swollen and partially stiff.

I prayed a simple prayer for her and told her to believe God, and went on my way.

78

Talk about excitement. The room was suddenly full of it. The little girl jumped up, began pumping her arms up and down. She threw her arms around her mother and cried for joy.

The mother was both happy and scared. "Honey, you mustn't do this," she cried. "Remember your rheumatic fever."

"But Mother, my rheumatic fever is gone! God has healed me! See! Look at my arms! I can raise them! Put your hand here on my heart! See! It is real quiet now!"

Then the mother became excited.

She was convinced it was a miracle.

But after they returned home, the mother began to lose her faith. The next day the little girl was jumping around all over the house, running and playing and having a good time.

"Honey, stop that. You know you can't do that."

"Mother, didn't you see me get healed last night?"

"Yes."

"Didn't you feel my heart? Didn't God heal me?"

"Yes."

"Then, Mother, I am all right. I can run and play."

"But, honey, what if it is not real?"

"Mother, all I have got to say to you is that you are just plain stupid!"

The mother started laughing and threw her arms around her child, and they had a merry time. Soon they were back to the meeting and the little girl came on the platform and showed herself to the people and testified to what Jesus had done for her.

*　*　*

You, too, may find that some of your friends will discourage you when you start trying to use your faith.

Not many will encourage you to turn your faith loose.

Not many will stand up and enthusiastically add their faith to yours.

Not many will say, "Well, everything has failed and now your only hope is God."

You will face many difficulties.

You may have to depend mainly on your own faith.

Just remember this about your faith—it is strong enough to bring deliverance to you.

80

Sometimes we forget what some of the people in the Bible had to go through for their deliverance.

They were criticized.

They were laughed at.

They were misunderstood.

They were rebuffed.

They were told it couldn't be done.

The case I have in mind now is the Syro-Phoenician woman told about in Matthew 15:22–28. (Please open your Bible and read this story.)

Her daughter was mentally ill.

Day after day she had watched her wasting away in mind and flesh.

Her child wasn't going to get well. Nothing in the world could cure her.

Then she heard about Jesus.

Jesus was a Jew.

But he was not like other men.

He went about "doing good, and healing all that were oppressed of the devil; for God was with him" (Acts 10:38).

He preached deliverance to the captives (Luke 4:18).

He gave people life and gave it to them more abundantly (John 10:10).

He was moved with compassion when he saw people afflicted and healed them (Mark 1:41).

He healed by the touch of his hand. By his word. By touching his clothes.

Thousands were healed by him. The blind. The deaf and dumb. The halt and maimed. Everyone who believed.

There was great enthusiasm among the people. His name was on every lip. Faith was high.

The Syro-Phoenician woman heard about Jesus.

But for her it would not be easy.

She was classed as a "Gentile dog."

She was not acceptable in Galilee where Jesus was healing the people.

Many would be against her.

None of her neighbors would encourage her to go.

It would take strong faith and great personal courage.

She would be humiliated and scorned.

But she felt she could endure anything if she could get her child healed.

When she arrived where Jesus was, she cried, "Oh, Lord, thou Son of David, my daughter is grievously vexed with a devil. Have mercy, Lord, and heal her."

He answered her not a word.

She turned from him to his disciples.

They turned their backs on her.

She came around in front of them pleading with them for help.

The disciples said to Jesus, "Send her away for she crieth after us."

Jesus answered, "I am not sent but to the lost sheep of the house of Israel."

The woman came up to Jesus, fell down before him and worshiped him.

"Lord, help me," she cried.

Jesus was deeply moved.

His compassion started flowing toward her.

He decided to put her to the acid test.

"It is not meet," he said, "to give the children's bread to dogs."

This means that the "children's bread" is healing for the bodies of God's children.

This woman was a sinner.

She was a "Gentile dog" who cared nothing about God and decent living.

"Truth, Lord," she said, admitting she was not a child of God nor was worthy of becoming one. "Yet the dogs eat of the crumbs which fall from their master's table."

She was referring to the little house dogs, common among the Jews. These little dogs were always under their master's table during mealtime. From time to time the children would take the crumbs from their plates and pitch them under the table to their little dogs.

If she cannot be his child and sit at the table with him eating the children's bread, then she wants to be like the little house dog and at least get the crumbs from the Master's table.

Jesus was astonished.

He was thrilled.

He had been searching for this kind of faith.

"Oh woman, great is thy faith," he cried, "be it unto thee even as thou wilt."

"And her daughter was made whole from that very hour."

This woman is one of the two people in the New Testament whom Jesus said had "great faith."

The other was the centurion (Matthew 8:5–13).

Everyone's faith can be great faith.

Great faith recognizes Jesus' power over sickness and disease.

It will press its way in to Jesus when others criticize, mock and scorn.

It refuses to be discouraged or dismayed.

It will not take no for an answer.

It will not quit.

It will fight its way through to the Lord of power and deliverance.

It will get results.

Are you having to go through opposition?

Are you being criticized or laughed at or scorned?

Do you feel it's just too difficult to press your way through?

Then pause a moment.

Think about the Syro-Phoenician woman.

Think about the little Canadian girl with rheumatic fever.

Think of these two cases, separated by almost two thousand years, and how they can be applied to your own case.

REMEMBER THESE THINGS

When no one else is interested in your healing, Jesus is.

Great faith will not take no for an answer.

Nobody nor anything can stand between you and deliverance if you are determined to use your faith.

The faith you have is sufficient. Put it into action and it will deliver you.

The children's bread is healing. If you are God's child, he wants you to be healed. If you are not his child, he wants you to be and will save you right now if you will believe.

CHAPTER VIII

How to Keep Your Healing

"SON, YOU BELIEVED GOD AND HE HEALED YOU," Mama said to me just after I was healed of tuberculosis and a stuttering tongue. "Now remember," she continued, "what you did to get your healing, you must continue to do to keep your healing."

That happened nearly 20 years ago, and I am still perfectly healed.

What are some of the things I have learned through the years to help keep one's healing?

First, make up your mind you are going to live a Christian life regardless of what happens to you. I am serving God, not because He healed my body, but because He saved my soul and because I love Him and His way of life. Jesus is not only my personal Savior but my daily example and ideal. I am trying to follow His steps.

87

Second, cultivate your faith, and it will grow stronger.

The law of life is that everything reproduces after its kind. Truth begets truth; lies beget lies; faith begets faith; fear begets fear.

As one's faith increases, God's power in his life increases. This has continually happened to me.

Third, seek a harmony with those people who have strong faith. Christ's mind is reproduced through the unity of two or more who are gathered together in Jesus' name (Matthew 18:19, 20). The union of two minds of faith brings forth a third mind, which is a composite of the two. My faith is always stronger when I am with a person or persons who also believe right.

Fourth, think positive thoughts about life.

I have never allowed my mind to entertain negative thoughts. For I firmly believe if I allowed myself to become negative in my thinking and believing, my afflictions would return to me. It took positive believing to get my lungs and tongue healed; it takes the same to keep them healed.

Fifth, in times of discouragement or loneliness or confusion, read your Bible constantly. It always helps to read the Bible. It helps more when you are in need of strength or courage or stronger faith.

88

At a time when you are tried, even the touch of the Bible is wonderful. I often take it to bed with me and sleep with it cradled in my arm. The feel of it gives me confidence for I know it is true and eternal. Things may be going to pieces all around, but the Word of God is sure and steadfast. It is an anchor to the soul.

The passage I read over and over when I feel weak is Luke 10:19. "Behold, I give unto you power . . . over all the power of the enemy: and nothing shall by any means hurt you." This always reads well when you are accosted by the enemy and have feelings of inadequacy.

When I feel bad in body or mind or spirit, and the devil would have me believe God was making me feel that way, I turn to Luke 9:56 and read it until Satan no longer can cause me to believe that. "The Son of man is not come to destroy men's lives, but to save them."

Anything that would destroy me, such as sickness, oppression or fear, are not sent by God. He came to save, not destroy.

And when I still need help along this line, John 10:10 supplies it fully. "The thief (Satan) cometh not, but for to steal, and to kill, and to destroy: I

89

am come that they might have life, and that they might have it more abundantly."

God wants us to be happy, normal and enjoy life more abundantly.

When I can't pay my bills, or acquire financial security, 3 John 2 always helps me. "Beloved, I wish above all things that thou mayest prosper." This is a verse I often read a dozen times without stopping. God is interested in our material needs and gives us His promise. "My God shall supply all your need according to His riches in glory by Christ Jesus" (Philippians 4:19).

Psalms 1, 23, 37, 91 are especially inspiring to me when I need strength and confidence, and I read them often.

Matthew 8 is another chapter I frequently read, especially in times of personal sickness or when I need healing faith for others.

All of us see things we should have, but which appear hopeless to us. Mark 9:23 is my verse for this. "If thou canst believe, all things are possible to him that believeth."

Reading the Bible like this, and having it near me all the time, helps me to think and believe in a positive manner. It strengthens my determination and increases my faith.

90

Sixth, go often to the house of God and hear a good anointed minister. "Faith cometh by hearing and hearing by the Word of God."

In a sense, you "hear the Word of God" as you read it. Nothing, however, can take the place of "hearing."

When the preacher is anointed by the Spirit of God, and is on fire, he handles the Word very skillfully. He seems to say just the right thing to help you believe and release your faith. He puts you in a better attitude, a faith-attitude. When you leave God's house for your home or job, you carry a new strength, an inner light, a deeper knowledge, a stronger determination and a greater faith.

I especially love the services of the church, and have found no substitute for the blessings of strength and help they bring to me.

Seventh, connect yourself with a cause that is greater than you are.

After my salvation and healing, I gave myself so completely to God that I lost my life. In losing it, I found it again. Many times I have quoted the poem that best illustrates how I feel about this:

I had walked life's way with an easy tread,
Had followed where comforts and pleasures led,

91

Until one day in a quiet place,
I met the Master face to face.

With station and rank and wealth for my goal,
Much thought for my body but none for my soul,
I entered to win in life's mad race,
When I met the Master face to face.

I met him and knew him and blushed to see,
That his eyes full of sorrow were fixed on me.
And I faltered and fell at his feet that day,
While my castles melted and vanished away.

Melted and vanished and in their place,
Naught else could I see, but my Master's face.
And I cried aloud, O, make me meet,
To follow the steps of thy wounded feet.

My thought is now for the souls of men.
I've lost my life to find it again.
E'er since that day in a quiet place,
I met the Master face to face.

Once there was a little boy who had a great desire to be a concert pianist. His parents, being poor, could not afford to send him to the great teachers.

Finally, however, when the child had progressed beyond all the local teachers, his parents took him to an old white-haired retired professor whose pupils had made him famous.

"I am too old to undertake this child's future," he declared as he refused the parents' plea.

"Would you please listen to him just once?" they pleaded.

The boy had played only a few seconds when the professor jumped to his feet, clapped his hands and cried, "He's got it, I will take him."

During the next few years the old professor carefully taught and guided the boy. He taught him not only the rudiments of music but the purpose of music itself. Music is the story of love and hate, of power and weakness, of honor and dishonor, of war and peace, of laughter and tears. It is all these translated into the readable script of life.

The boy learned well. Then came the day of his debut. News had traveled far and wide that a great new musician was rising. That night the hall was filled with eager music lovers.

Before the concert was half through, the boy had captured the hearts of his audience. By the time he reached his climax they were cheering wildly. Men and women rushed to the stage and threw their purses at his feet.

Not once did the young boy look at his audience.

Instead he kept his eyes on the balcony. There the old white-haired music professor was sitting and nodding his head and saying, "You are on the right track my boy, just keep it up."

The writer to the Hebrews said, "Looking unto Jesus, the author and finisher of your faith" (Hebrews 12:2).

Somewhere up on the balcony of heaven Jesus sits watching us. He is nodding and saying, "You are on the right track, just keep it up."

Keeping our eyes on Jesus, that is the secret.

THE END